This Planner Belongs To:

Plantastic Press

2020

January

S	M	T	W	T	F	S
			1	2	3	4
5	6	7	8	9	10	11
12	13	14	15	16	17	18
19	20	21	22	23	24	25
26	27	28	29	30	31	

February

S	M	T	W	T	F	S
						1
2	3	4	5	6	7	8
9	10	11	12	13	14	15
16	17	18	19	20	21	22
23	24	25	26	27	28	29

March

S	M	T	W	T	F	S
1	2	3	4	5	6	7
8	9	10	11	12	13	14
15	16	17	18	19	20	21
22	23	24	25	26	27	28
29	30	31				

April

S	M	T	W	T	F	S
			1	2	3	4
5	6	7	8	9	10	11
12	13	14	15	16	17	18
19	20	21	22	23	24	25
26	27	28	29	30		

May

S	M	T	W	T	F	S
					1	2
3	4	5	6	7	8	9
10	11	12	13	14	15	16
17	18	19	20	21	22	23
24	25	26	27	28	29	30
31						

June

S	M	T	W	T	F	S
	1	2	3	4	5	6
7	8	9	10	11	12	13
14	15	16	17	18	19	20
21	22	23	24	25	26	27
28	29	30				

July

S	M	T	W	T	F	S
			1	2	3	4
5	6	7	8	9	10	11
12	13	14	15	16	17	18
19	20	21	22	23	24	25
26	27	28	29	30	31	

August

S	M	T	W	T	F	S
						1
2	3	4	5	6	7	8
9	10	11	12	13	14	15
16	17	18	19	20	21	22
23	24	25	26	27	28	29
30	31					

September

S	M	T	W	T	F	S
		1	2	3	4	5
6	7	8	9	10	11	12
13	14	15	16	17	18	19
20	21	22	23	24	25	26
27	28	29	30			

October

S	M	T	W	T	F	S
				1	2	3
4	5	6	7	8	9	10
11	12	13	14	15	16	17
18	19	20	21	22	23	24
25	26	27	28	29	30	31

November

S	M	T	W	T	F	S
1	2	3	4	5	6	7
8	9	10	11	12	13	14
15	16	17	18	19	20	21
22	23	24	25	26	27	28
29	30					

December

S	M	T	W	T	F	S
		1	2	3	4	5
6	7	8	9	10	11	12
13	14	15	16	17	18	19
20	21	22	23	24	25	26
27	28	29	30	31		

December

Week 1

12/30/19 - 01/05/20

○ 30. MONDAY

○ 31. TUESDAY

○ 1. WEDNESDAY

○ 2. THURSDAY

○ 3. FRIDAY

○ 4. SATURDAY / 5. SUNDAY

PRIORITIES

TO DO

January

Week 2

01/06/20 - 01/12/20

○ 6. MONDAY

PRIORITIES

○ 7. TUESDAY

○ 8. WEDNESDAY

TO DO

○ 9. THURSDAY

○ 10. FRIDAY

○ 11. SATURDAY / 12. SUNDAY

January

Week 3

01/13/20 - 01/19/20

◯ 13. MONDAY

PRIORITIES

◯ 14. TUESDAY

◯ 15. WEDNESDAY

TO DO

◯ 16. THURSDAY

◯ 17. FRIDAY

◯ 18. SATURDAY / 19. SUNDAY

January

Week 4

01/20/20 - 01/26/20

○ 20. MONDAY

PRIORITIES

○ 21. TUESDAY

○ 22. WEDNESDAY

TO DO

○ 23. THURSDAY

○ 24. FRIDAY

○ 25. SATURDAY / 26. SUNDAY

January

Week 5

01/27/20 - 02/02/20

○ 27. MONDAY

○ 28. TUESDAY

○ 29. WEDNESDAY

○ 30. THURSDAY

○ 31. FRIDAY

○ 1. SATURDAY / 2. SUNDAY

PRIORITIES

TO DO

February

Week 6

02/03/20 - 02/09/20

3. MONDAY

PRIORITIES

4. TUESDAY

5. WEDNESDAY

TO DO

6. THURSDAY

7. FRIDAY

8. SATURDAY / 9. SUNDAY

February

Week 7

02/10/20 - 02/16/20

- ○ 10. MONDAY
- ○ 11. TUESDAY
- ○ 12. WEDNESDAY
- ○ 13. THURSDAY
- ○ 14. FRIDAY
- ○ 15. SATURDAY / 16. SUNDAY

PRIORITIES

TO DO

February

Week 8

02/17/20 - 02/23/20

- [ ] 17. MONDAY

PRIORITIES

- [ ] 18. TUESDAY

- [ ] 19. WEDNESDAY

TO DO

- [ ] 20. THURSDAY

- [ ] 21. FRIDAY

- [ ] 22. SATURDAY / 23. SUNDAY

February

Week 9

02/24/20 - 03/01/20

○ 24. MONDAY

PRIORITIES

○ 25. TUESDAY

○ 26. WEDNESDAY

TO DO

○ 27. THURSDAY

○ 28. FRIDAY

○ 29. SATURDAY / 1. SUNDAY

March

Week 10

03/02/20 - 03/08/20

○ 2. MONDAY

PRIORITIES

○ 3. TUESDAY

○ 4. WEDNESDAY

TO DO

○ 5. THURSDAY

○ 6. FRIDAY

○ 7. SATURDAY / 8. SUNDAY

March

Week 11

03/09/20 - 03/15/20

○ 9. MONDAY

PRIORITIES

○ 10. TUESDAY

○ 11. WEDNESDAY

TO DO

○ 12. THURSDAY

○ 13. FRIDAY

○ 14. SATURDAY / 15. SUNDAY

March

Week 12

03/16/20 - 03/22/20

16. MONDAY

17. TUESDAY

18. WEDNESDAY

19. THURSDAY

20. FRIDAY

21. SATURDAY / 22. SUNDAY

PRIORITIES

TO DO

March

Week 13

03/23/20 - 03/29/20

○ 23. MONDAY

○ 24. TUESDAY

○ 25. WEDNESDAY

○ 26. THURSDAY

○ 27. FRIDAY

○ 28. SATURDAY / 29. SUNDAY

PRIORITIES

TO DO

March

Week 14

03/30/20 - 04/05/20

○ 30. MONDAY

○ 31. TUESDAY

○ 1. WEDNESDAY

○ 2. THURSDAY

○ 3. FRIDAY

○ 4. SATURDAY / 5. SUNDAY

PRIORITIES

TO DO

April

Week 15

04/06/20 - 04/12/20

○ 6. MONDAY

PRIORITIES

○ 7. TUESDAY

○ 8. WEDNESDAY

TO DO

○ 9. THURSDAY

○ 10. FRIDAY

○ 11. SATURDAY / 12. SUNDAY

April

Week 16

04/13/20 - 04/19/20

○ 13. MONDAY

○ 14. TUESDAY

○ 15. WEDNESDAY

○ 16. THURSDAY

○ 17. FRIDAY

○ 18. SATURDAY / 19. SUNDAY

PRIORITIES

TO DO

April

Week 17

04/20/20 - 04/26/20

20. MONDAY

PRIORITIES

21. TUESDAY

22. WEDNESDAY

TO DO

23. THURSDAY

24. FRIDAY

25. SATURDAY / 26. SUNDAY

April

Week 18

04/27/20 - 05/03/20

○ 27. MONDAY

PRIORITIES

○ 28. TUESDAY

○ 29. WEDNESDAY

TO DO

○ 30. THURSDAY

○ 1. FRIDAY

○ 2. SATURDAY / 3. SUNDAY

May

Week 19

05/04/20 - 05/10/20

○ 4. MONDAY

PRIORITIES

○ 5. TUESDAY

○ 6. WEDNESDAY

TO DO

○ 7. THURSDAY

○ 8. FRIDAY

○ 9. SATURDAY / 10. SUNDAY

May

Week 20

05/11/20 - 05/17/20

○ 11. MONDAY

PRIORITIES

○ 12. TUESDAY

○ 13. WEDNESDAY

TO DO

○ 14. THURSDAY

○ 15. FRIDAY

○ 16. SATURDAY / 17. SUNDAY

May

Week 21

05/18/20 - 05/24/20

18. MONDAY

19. TUESDAY

20. WEDNESDAY

21. THURSDAY

22. FRIDAY

23. SATURDAY / 24. SUNDAY

PRIORITIES

TO DO

May

Week 22

05/25/20 - 05/31/20

25. MONDAY

26. TUESDAY

27. WEDNESDAY

28. THURSDAY

29. FRIDAY

30. SATURDAY / 31. SUNDAY

PRIORITIES

TO DO

June

Week 23

06/01/20 - 06/07/20

○ 1. MONDAY

PRIORITIES

○ 2. TUESDAY

○ 3. WEDNESDAY

TO DO

○ 4. THURSDAY

○ 5. FRIDAY

○ 6. SATURDAY / 7. SUNDAY

June

Week 24

06/08/20 - 06/14/20

8. MONDAY

9. TUESDAY

10. WEDNESDAY

11. THURSDAY

12. FRIDAY

13. SATURDAY / 14. SUNDAY

PRIORITIES

TO DO

June

Week 25

06/15/20 - 06/21/20

○ 15. MONDAY

○ 16. TUESDAY

○ 17. WEDNESDAY

○ 18. THURSDAY

○ 19. FRIDAY

○ 20. SATURDAY / 21. SUNDAY

PRIORITIES

TO DO

June

Week 26

06/22/20 - 06/28/20

○ 22. MONDAY

PRIORITIES

○ 23. TUESDAY

○ 24. WEDNESDAY

TO DO

○ 25. THURSDAY

○ 26. FRIDAY

○ 27. SATURDAY / 28. SUNDAY

June

Week 27

06/29/20 - 07/05/20

○ 29. MONDAY

PRIORITIES

○ 30. TUESDAY

○ 1. WEDNESDAY

TO DO

○ 2. THURSDAY

○ 3. FRIDAY

○ 4. SATURDAY / 5. SUNDAY

July

Week 28

07/06/20 - 07/12/20

6. MONDAY

PRIORITIES

7. TUESDAY

8. WEDNESDAY

TO DO

9. THURSDAY

10. FRIDAY

11. SATURDAY / 12. SUNDAY

July

Week 29

07/13/20 - 07/19/20

- [ ] 13. MONDAY

- [ ] 14. TUESDAY

- [ ] 15. WEDNESDAY

- [ ] 16. THURSDAY

- [ ] 17. FRIDAY

- [ ] 18. SATURDAY / 19. SUNDAY

PRIORITIES

TO DO

July

Week 30

07/20/20 - 07/26/20

20. MONDAY

PRIORITIES

21. TUESDAY

22. WEDNESDAY

TO DO

23. THURSDAY

24. FRIDAY

25. SATURDAY / 26. SUNDAY

July

Week 31

07/27/20 - 08/02/20

○ 27. MONDAY

○ 28. TUESDAY

○ 29. WEDNESDAY

○ 30. THURSDAY

○ 31. FRIDAY

○ 1. SATURDAY / 2. SUNDAY

PRIORITIES

TO DO

August

Week 32

08/03/20 - 08/09/20

3. MONDAY

PRIORITIES

4. TUESDAY

5. WEDNESDAY

TO DO

6. THURSDAY

7. FRIDAY

8. SATURDAY / 9. SUNDAY

August

Week 33

08/10/20 - 08/16/20

○ 10. MONDAY

PRIORITIES

○ 11. TUESDAY

○ 12. WEDNESDAY

TO DO

○ 13. THURSDAY

○ 14. FRIDAY

○ 15. SATURDAY / 16. SUNDAY

August

Week 34

08/17/20 - 08/23/20

17. MONDAY

PRIORITIES

18. TUESDAY

19. WEDNESDAY

TO DO

20. THURSDAY

21. FRIDAY

22. SATURDAY / 23 SUNDAY

August

Week 35

08/24/20 - 08/30/20

○ 24. MONDAY

PRIORITIES

○ 25. TUESDAY

○ 26. WEDNESDAY

TO DO

○ 27. THURSDAY

○ 28. FRIDAY

○ 29. SATURDAY / 30. SUNDAY

August

Week 36

08/31/20 - C9/06/20

○ 31. MONDAY

PRIORITIES

○ 1. TUESDAY

○ 2. WEDNESDAY

TO DO

○ 3. THURSDAY

○ 4. FRIDAY

○ 5. SATURDAY / 6. SUNDAY

September

Week 37

09/07/20 - 09/13/20

○ 7. MONDAY

PRIORITIES

○ 8. TUESDAY

○ 9. WEDNESDAY

TO DO

○ 10. THURSDAY

○ 11. FRIDAY

○ 12. SATURDAY / 13. SUNDAY

September

Week 38

09/14/20 - 09/20/20

- [ ] 14. MONDAY

- [ ] 15. TUESDAY

- [ ] 16. WEDNESDAY

- [ ] 17. THURSDAY

- [ ] 18. FRIDAY

- [ ] 19. SATURDAY / 20. SUNDAY

PRIORITIES

TO DO

September

Week 39

09/21/20 - 09/27/20

○ 21. MONDAY

PRIORITIES

○ 22. TUESDAY

○ 23. WEDNESDAY

TO DO

○ 24. THURSDAY

○ 25. FRIDAY

○ 26. SATURDAY / 27. SUNDAY

September

Week 40

09/28/20 - 10/04/20

○ 28. MONDAY

PRIORITIES

○ 29. TUESDAY

○ 30. WEDNESDAY

TO DO

○ 1. THURSDAY

○ 2. FRIDAY

○ 3. SATURDAY / 4. SUNDAY

October

Week 41

10/05/20 - 10/11/20

○ 5. MONDAY

○ 6. TUESDAY

○ 7. WEDNESDAY

○ 8. THURSDAY

○ 9. FRIDAY

○ 10. SATURDAY / 11. SUNDAY

PRIORITIES

TO DO

October

Week 42

10/12/20 - 10/18/20

○ 12. MONDAY

PRIORITIES

○ 13. TUESDAY

○ 14. WEDNESDAY

TO DO

○ 15. THURSDAY

○ 16. FRIDAY

○ 17. SATURDAY / 18. SUNDAY

October

Week 43

10/19/20 - 10/25/20

○ 19. MONDAY

○ 20. TUESDAY

○ 21. WEDNESDAY

○ 22. THURSDAY

○ 23. FRIDAY

○ 24. SATURDAY / 25. SUNDAY

PRIORITIES

TO DO

October

Week 44

10/26/20 - 11/01/20

26. MONDAY

PRIORITIES

27. TUESDAY

28. WEDNESDAY

TO DO

29. THURSDAY

30. FRIDAY

31. SATURDAY / 1. SUNDAY

November

Week 45

11/02/20 - 11/08/20

◯ 2. MONDAY

PRIORITIES

◯ 3. TUESDAY

◯ 4. WEDNESDAY

TO DO

◯ 5. THURSDAY

◯ 6. FRIDAY

◯ 7. SATURDAY / 8. SUNDAY

November

Week 46

11/09/20 - 11/15/20

○ 9. MONDAY

○ 10. TUESDAY

○ 11. WEDNESDAY

○ 12. THURSDAY

○ 13. FRIDAY

○ 14. SATURDAY / 15 SUNDAY

PRIORITIES

TO DO

November

Week 47

11/16/20 - 11/22/20

16. MONDAY

PRIORITIES

17. TUESDAY

18. WEDNESDAY

TO DO

19. THURSDAY

20. FRIDAY

21. SATURDAY / 22. SUNDAY

November

Week 48

11/23/20 - 11/29/20

23. MONDAY

PRIORITIES

24. TUESDAY

25. WEDNESDAY

TO DO

26. THURSDAY

27. FRIDAY

28. SATURDAY / 29. SUNDAY

November

Week 49

11/30/20 - 12/06/20

- [ ] 30. MONDAY

PRIORITIES

- [ ] 1. TUESDAY

- [ ] 2. WEDNESDAY

TO DO

- [ ] 3. THURSDAY

- [ ] 4. FRIDAY

- [ ] 5. SATURDAY / 6. SUNDAY

December

Week 50

12/07/20 - 12/13/20

○ 7. MONDAY

PRIORITIES

○ 8. TUESDAY

○ 9. WEDNESDAY

TO DO

○ 10. THURSDAY

○ 11. FRIDAY

○ 12. SATURDAY / 13. SUNDAY

December

Week 51

12/14/20 - 12/20/20

○ 14. MONDAY

PRIORITIES

○ 15. TUESDAY

○ 16. WEDNESDAY

TO DO

○ 17. THURSDAY

○ 18. FRIDAY

○ 19. SATURDAY / 20. SUNDAY

December

Week 52

12/21/20 - 12/27/20

○ 21. MONDAY

○ 22. TUESDAY

○ 23. WEDNESDAY

○ 24. THURSDAY

○ 25. FRIDAY

○ 26. SATURDAY / 27. SUNDAY

PRIORITIES

TO DO

December

Week 53

12/28/20 - 01/03/21

○ 28. MONDAY

○ 29. TUESDAY

○ 30. WEDNESDAY

○ 31. THURSDAY

○ 1. FRIDAY

○ 2. SATURDAY / 3. SUNDAY

PRIORITIES

TO DO

Printed in Great Britain
by Amazon

33523902R00061